Date Due			
DEC 1 1982			

Ridiman, Bob
    What Is A Shadow?

WHAT IS A SHADOW?

A Second Book of Simple Science Fun

by Bob Ridiman

Experiences with
Gravity, Shadows,
Mirrors and
Electricity

A Humpty Dumpty Book

Parents' Magazine Press / New York

Library of Congress Cataloging in Publication Data
Ridiman, Bob.
    What is a shadow?

    (A Humpty Dumpty book)
    SUMMARY: Simple experiments demonstrate some effects
and uses of electricity, shadows, mirrors, and gravity.
    1. Science — Experiments — Juvenile literature.
[1. Science — Experiments] I. Title.
Q163.R5   530'.028   73-4368
ISBN 0-8193-0688-6
ISBN 0-8193-0689-4 (lib. bdg.)

GRAVITY

SHADOWS

MIRRORS

ELECTRICITY

GRAVITY

holds you on the earth

The earth pulls
everything
on it or near it.
The pull of the
earth is called
GRAVITY.

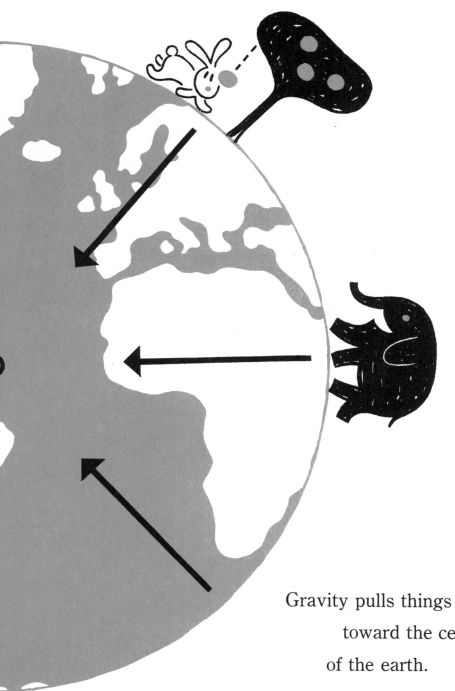

Gravity pulls things
toward the center
of the earth.

A SCALE tells
you how much
the earth is
pulling something.

The earth is pulling

the panda with a force of 3 pounds.

How much is the
earth pulling YOU?
(How much do you weigh?)

Weigh yourself alone.
Weigh yourself with your dog.
How much does your dog weigh?

Copy TOM TUMBLER on cardboard.

cut off ⅓ of a ping pong ball

half-fill this part with clay

stand Tom in the clay

Gravity makes Tom bob right up
when you push him over.

The earth is pulling
his heavy clay bottom.

Air reduces the pull of gravity.

Take two pieces
of paper the same
size. Crumple one
into a small ball.

Drop both pieces
at the same time.
Which paper reaches the floor first?

The ball of paper falls faster than the flat paper.

The flat paper
is held back by
more air than the
small paper ball.

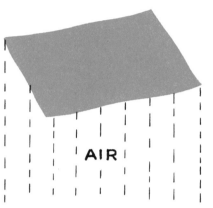

Air slows falling objects.

You can make a PAPER HELICOPTER.

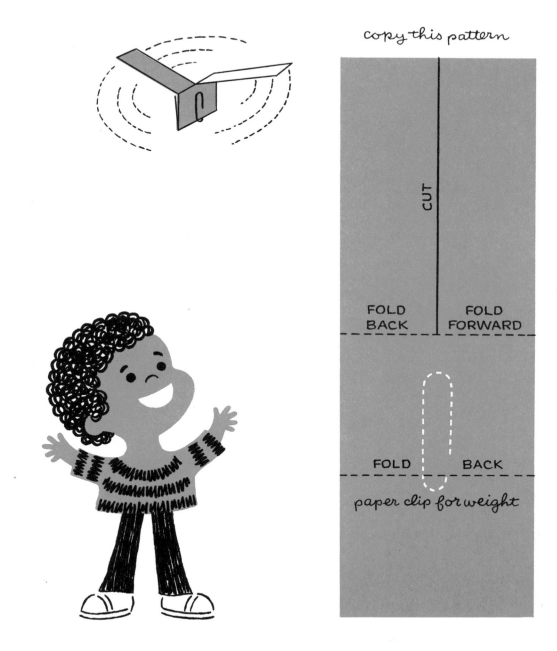

copy this pattern

CUT

FOLD BACK   FOLD FORWARD

FOLD   BACK

paper clip for weight

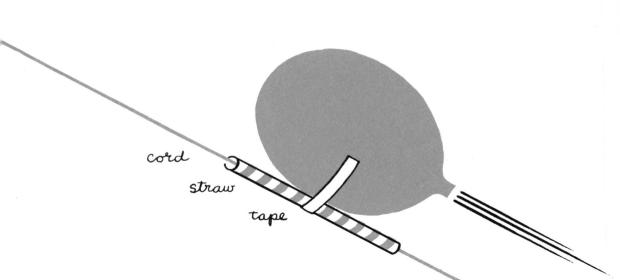

cord
straw
tape

LAUNCH A BALLOON ROCKET.

Air in the balloon
pushes in *all* directions.
Air pushing backward
gets out. Air pushing
forward moves the
balloon ahead.

Jet planes and rockets
    overcome the pull of gravity.

Hot gasses act like
    the air in the balloon
    and push jet planes
    and rockets forward.

launching pad

How does a big steel boat overcome

the pull of gravity and float?

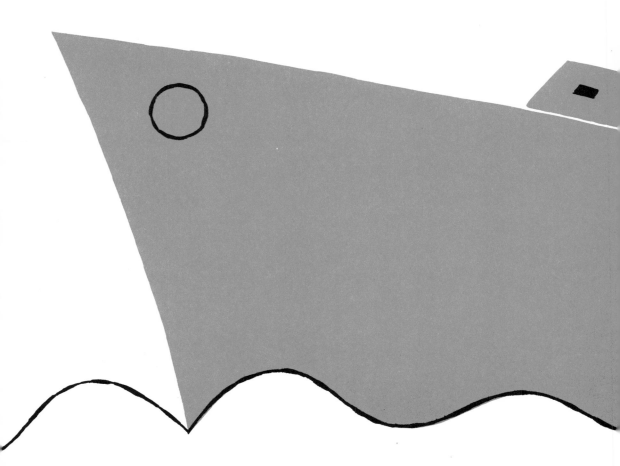

Why does a little steel nail sink?

Drop a large lump
of modeling clay
into a pan of water.

The lump
SINKS.

The lump of clay sinks because it weighs *more*
than the water it takes the place of, or DISPLACES.

Now shape *the same lump of clay* into a
boat with a flat bottom and high sides.

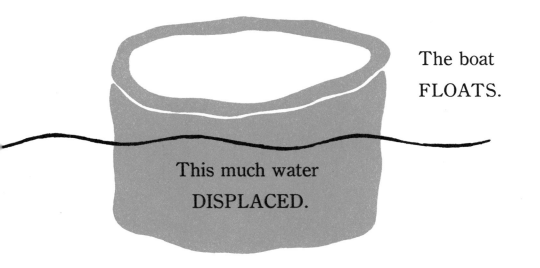

The boat
FLOATS.

This much water
DISPLACED.

The clay boat floats because the weight
of the displaced water pushing *up* equals
the weight of the boat pushing *down*.

How many marbles

will your boat hold

before it sinks?

SHADOWS
are made when objects block light

The sun shines *on* you
and *around* you
but not *through* you.

Your body blocks the light
and makes your shadow.

In early morning and late afternoon
the sun is low in the sky.

Your shadow is long and skinny.

Where is the sun
when your shadow
is short and fat?

Make this SHADOW COMPASS on a sunny day.

tall stick

stone at end of shadow

15 minutes later

another stone at end of new shadow

EAST

An arrow drawn from the first stone to the second points EAST.

You can see what makes an ECLIPSE OF THE SUN.

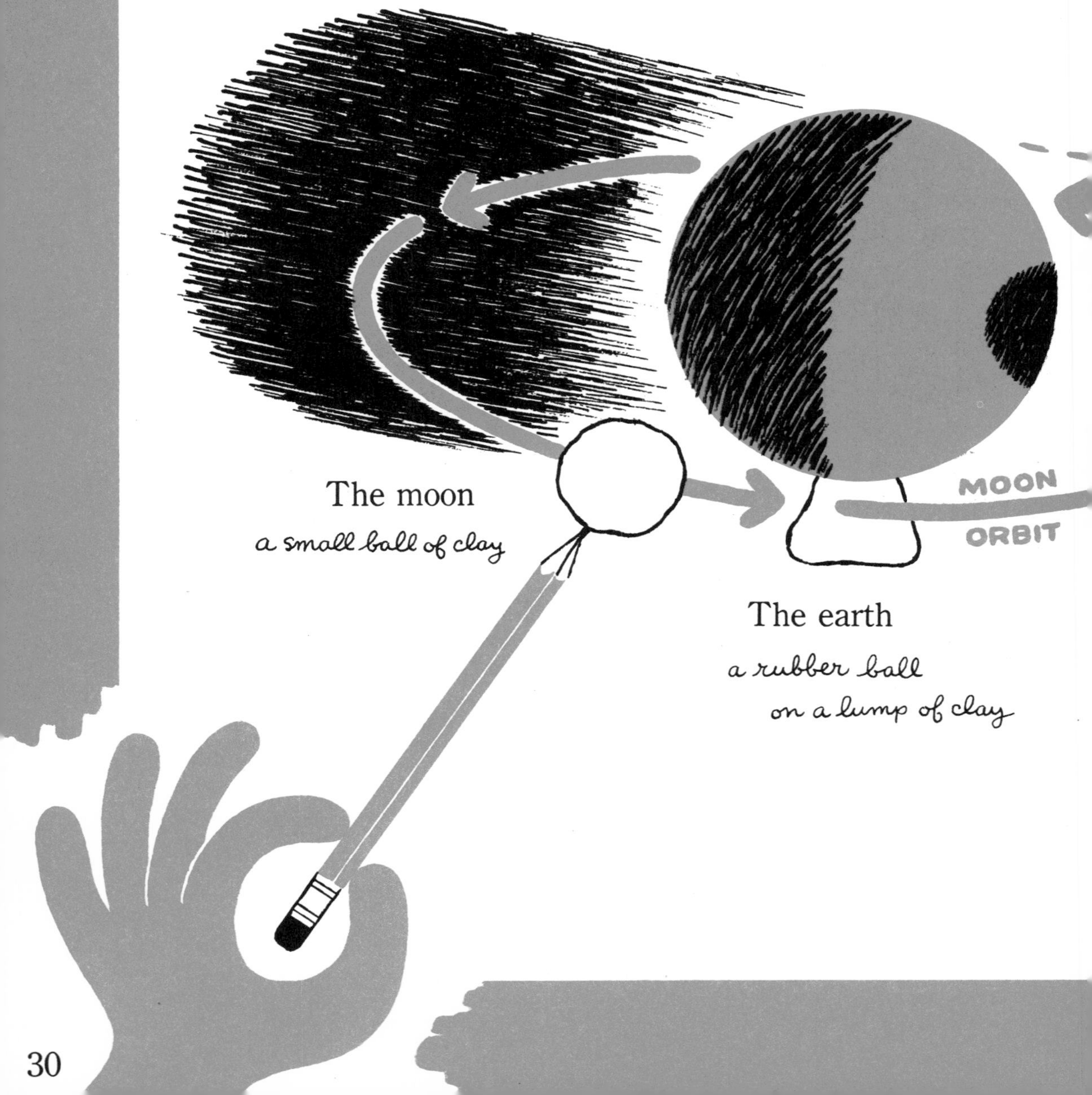

The moon
a small ball of clay

MOON
ORBIT

The earth
*a rubber ball
on a lump of clay*

Move the moon in orbit until it is between
the sun and the earth. The sunlight is blocked,
or *eclipsed*, by the moon. The moon's
shadow falls on the earth. This is an
eclipse of the sun, or *solar* eclipse.

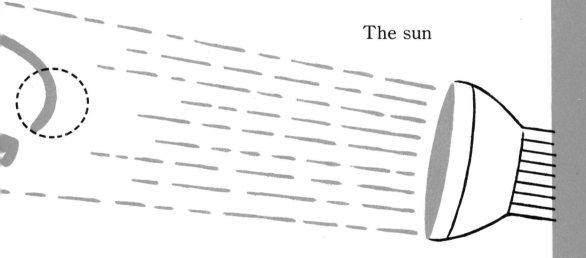

The sun

Move the moon in orbit until it is
in the earth's shadow. This is an
eclipse of the moon, or *lunar* eclipse.

A shadow tells time on this
PAPER PLATE SUNDIAL.

Push a pencil through
the center of an
upside-down paper plate.

Every hour number
the pencil's shadow.
Don't move your sundial.

The next day it will tell you the time.

point in ground

SHADE is a
cool shadow
on a hot day.

SHADOW ANIMALS are fun to make.

dinosaur

ostrich

kangaroo

MIRRORS

change the way you see things

You can see over and around with a PERISCOPE.

Make your own PERISCOPE with milk cartons.

Fix two
milk cartons
like this:

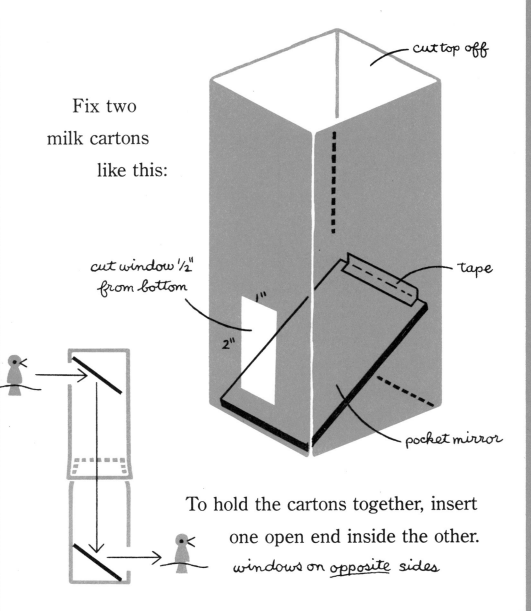

cut top off

cut window ½"
from bottom

1"

2"

tape

pocket mirror

To hold the cartons together, insert
one open end inside the other.

*windows on **opposite** sides*

You can see over things.

39

You can see around corners.

You can see behind you

switch the cartons
so the windows
are on the _same_ side

Everything looks backwards in a mirror.

When you raise one
hand, your reflection
or *mirror image* seems
to raise the other hand.

You can see many mirror images.

2 pocket mirrors
hinged with
transparent tape

button

Move the ends of the mirrors

towards you. How many mirror

images of the button do you see?

ELECTRICITY

is everywhere in everything

There is STATIC ELECTRICITY,
or electricity *at rest*,
in everything in the world...

in birds
and trees
and clouds,

in lions
and pumpkins
and worms.

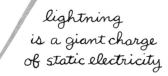

lightning
is a giant charge
of static electricity

There's even
electricity in YOU!

Combing *moves* static
electricity from your hair
to the comb, filling or
charging it electrically.

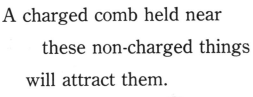
thin stream
of water

A charged comb held near
these non-charged things
will attract them.

small bits
of paper

thread snake

Charge a balloon. Rub it
on a lion. A cat or woolen
sweater will do instead.

The charged balloon is attracted
to the non-charged wall.

Is there electricity
in a wooden chair?

Electricity works for us only when it is *moving*.

CURRENT ELECTRICITY
flows steadily through wires
from the power plant where
it is produced, or *generated*.

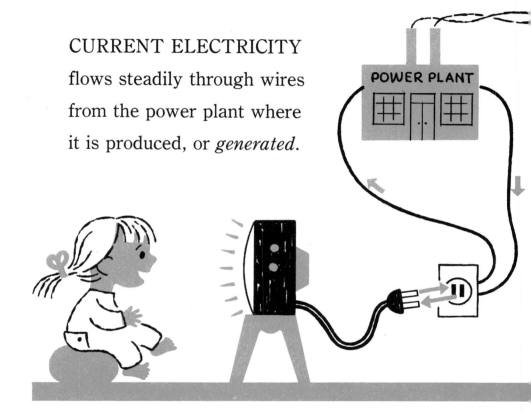

The electricity flows in a *circuit*, or round trip,
from the power plant to your house, and back
to the power plant. The electricity that is *used*
does not return to the power plant.

Here's an ELECTRIC CIRCUIT you can make
with a *portable* power plant—a BATTERY.

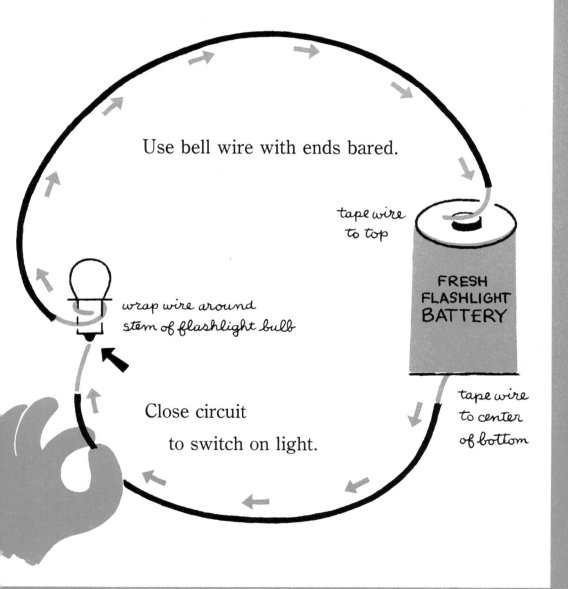

Use bell wire with ends bared.

tape wire
to top

FRESH
FLASHLIGHT
BATTERY

wrap wire around
stem of flashlight bulb

Close circuit
to switch on light.

tape wire
to center
of bottom

Electricity can
make magnets that
turn *on* and *off*.

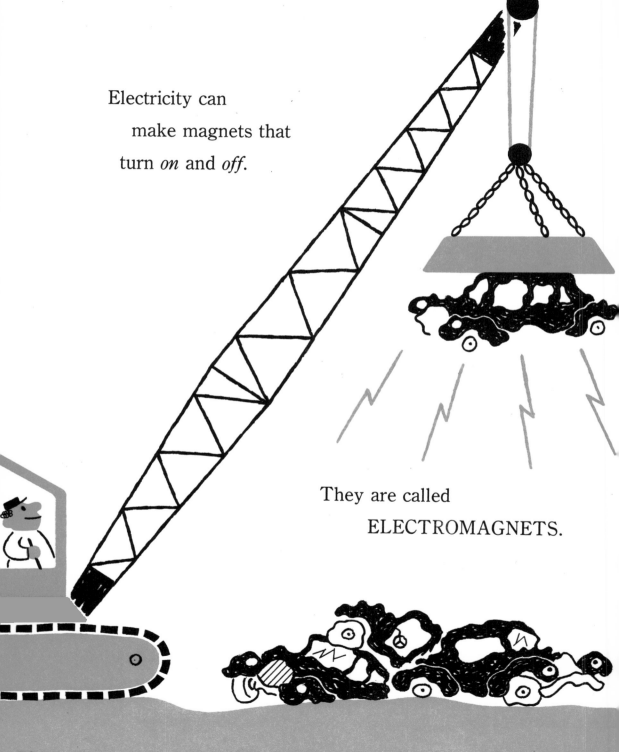

They are called
ELECTROMAGNETS.

You can make your own ELECTROMAGNET.

Electricity moving through wire
coiled around a nail makes
the nail an electromagnet.

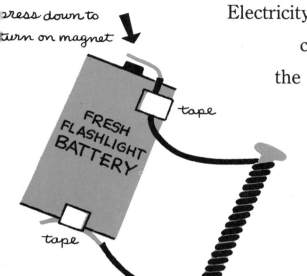

press down to turn on magnet

tape

FRESH FLASHLIGHT BATTERY

tape

wind 2 feet of bell wire
around a large nail—
bare ends of wire

How many paper clips
can your electromagnet
pick up? Can it pick up
thumbtacks, or an eraser?

BOB RIDIMAN was born in Elmira, New York and grew up in Cincinnati, Ohio, where he graduated from the Ohio Mechanics Institute. After a number of years working in advertising as an artist and art director, he now works as a freelance artist, painter and silversmith. He has contributed many simple, clearly illustrated science activities to *Humpty Dumpty's Magazine*. This is Mr. Ridiman's second collection of science activities for Parents' Magazine Press, his first being SIMPLE SCIENCE FUN, *Experiences with Light, Sound, Air and Water.*